How to be a
Ballerina

This is a Parragon Publishing Book
This edition published in 2004

Parragon Publishing
Queen Street House,
4 Queen Street,
Bath, BA1 1HE, UK

Printed in China
ISBN 1-40541-296-8

How to be a Ballerina

p

Written by Caroline Repchuk ◆ Illustrated by Fran Thatcher

Bella Ballerina

Bella looked around nervously at the other girls in her class. It was their first day at ballet school, and they were about to meet their teacher, the legendary Miss Meanie.

Rumor had it that she ate up bad little ballerinas for breakfast. If they were going to keep on her good side, they'd have to stay on their toes!

"Good morning, girls!"
Miss Meanie strode
into the dance
studio.
Everyone
sprang to attention.
"By the time I have finished,
I will make ballerinas of every
last one of you. And I will not
tolerate sloppiness like that!"
Bella cringed and
blushed scarlet as Miss Meanie
pointed to Bella's shoe ribbon,
which was dangling untied.
It looked like she had started
on the wrong foot!

Neat and Tidy

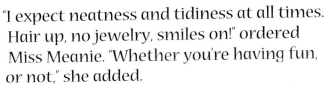

"I expect neatness and tidiness at all times. Hair up, no jewelry, smiles on!" ordered Miss Meanie. "Whether you're having fun, or not," she added.

Just in case anyone needed reminding, they ran through the proper way to tie shoe ribbons ...

Preparing for Class

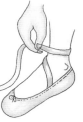

1. Keep your foot flat on the floor. Pass the inside ribbon across, around your ankle, and to the back again.

2. Cross the outside ribbon over the first one, and round your ankle.

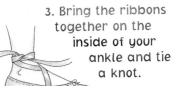

3. Bring the ribbons together on the inside of your ankle and tie a knot.

4. Tuck in the ends neatly.

In ballet class, your hair should always be tidy, and either put up in a bun, or pinned back securely. Jewelry must be taken off, as it could get caught, scratch someone, or snag clothes.

Class Act

"Becoming a ballet dancer takes hard work, dedication, and discipline," declared Miss Meanie. "Which means paying attention in class, Bella!"

Bella, who had been watching the birds, quickly swung her head to face the front. Uh-oh—in trouble again!

Take Your Positions

"Let's practice the positions of the arms and feet now, girls," instructed Miss Meanie. "Not so wild with your arms this time, Bella, you don't want to hit someone!"

Foot Positions

1st

2nd

"And you must keep your whole leg turned out at the hip, not just your foot. Remember, practice makes perfect!"

3rd

4th

5th

11

Spinning Around

"Let's try some pirouettes now girls," said Miss Meanie. "You can go first, Bella."

Bella floated across the floor on the tip of her toes, feeling as light and delicate as a feather. She spun into a perfect pirouette—then crashed in a heap on the floor!

"Sorry Miss Meanie," she mumbled.

"I told you to keep your eye on something as you turned," said Miss Meanie.

"I did," said Bella, "I kept my eye on the cat, but he moved!"

Spinning and Spotting

Dancers avoid getting giddy
by "spotting"—looking at a fixed
spot, then whipping their head round
quickly to find the spot again.

13

Partner Work

"Partner work now!" said Miss Meanie. "Bella, you're with Boris." Bella waited with baited breath to meet her new partner.

Which of the tall, handsome boys would it be?

Then a short clumsy-looking fellow stepped out from behind the others.

"Hello," he said. "I'm Boris." Bella's heart sank.

"A perfect match!" beamed Miss Meanie.

Without Words

"In ballet, we must learn to use gestures and expressions to convey our feelings," advised Miss Meanie. "I see you are leaving your partner in no doubt about yours, Bella!" she added.

Bella blushed deep pink again, put her hands back in first position, and her tongue back in her mouth!

Telling the Story

Mime is an important part of ballet, and is used to convey feelings as well as the plot, especially in the older traditional ballets such as "Swan Lake" and "The Sleeping Beauty." Each gesture has its own particular meaning:

Baby　　**Beg**　　**Sleep**　　**Kill**

Fright　　**Sorrow**　　**Love**　　**Hear**

Tales from the Ballet

"These are some of the great ballets you may have the pleasure of dancing in, if you ever perfect your pirouettes!" sighed Miss Meanie.

Swan Lake

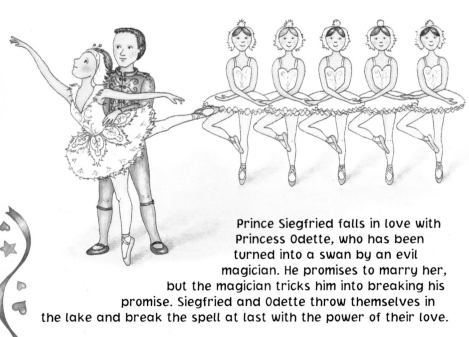

Prince Siegfried falls in love with Princess Odette, who has been turned into a swan by an evil magician. He promises to marry her, but the magician tricks him into breaking his promise. Siegfried and Odette throw themselves in the lake and break the spell at last with the power of their love.

Coppelia

Franz and Swanhilda live in a small town, where the toymaker Coppelius is trying to create a doll with a soul, called Coppelia. Franz falls in love with her, making Swanhilda jealous. Disguised as the doll, Swanhilda dances, then winds up the clockwork toys. The toys escape, leaving the toymaker heartbroken.

The Nutcracker

Clara is given a nutcracker for Christmas in the shape of a soldier. That night, her gifts grow huge and come to life. The Nutcracker battles the evil Mouse King, who changes into a prince. He takes her on a magical journey, where she meets the Snow Queen and the Sugar Plum Fairy.

The Sleeping Beauty

"Well, class, it's the moment you've all been waiting for!" announced Miss Meanie. "I am delighted to tell you that your first performance is to be the classic fairytale ballet, "The Sleeping Beauty."

Prologue

The fairies bring gifts to the royal christening. Carabosse, the bad fairy, is angry at being left out, and casts a spell. Princess Aurora will prick her finger on a spindle and die.

Act 1

Princess Aurora pricks her finger on a spindle and collapses. The Lilac Fairy changes the spell so the princess is not dead, but in a deep sleep.

Act 2

Prince Florimund finds the castle and wakes Princess Aurora with a kiss.

Act 3

The wedding of Prince Florimund and Princess Aurora, with entertainment from Puss in Boots and the White Cat.

"This ballet has all the ingredients of a great fairytale—a king and queen, good and bad fairies, a beautiful princess and a brave, handsome prince," declared Miss Meanie.

Shall We Dance?

The class fell silent as Miss Meanie chose who would dance each part in the ballet.

"Bella and Boris, you are to dance the leading roles!" she announced. The pair looked at each other in horror and amazement!

"Yes, yes!" snapped Miss Meanie. "I know you are hardly star-crossed lovers, but despite that, you do actually dance very well together!"

The Sleeping Beauty

Behind the Scenes

While Bella and Boris practiced intensely for their leading roles, plenty of hard work was going on behind the scenes, too.

Musicians in the orchestra practice to accompany the ballet with beautiful music.

Stage technicians organize sound, lighting, scenery, props, and special effects. A large theater may have a team of more than one hundred people.

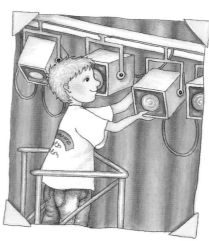

Set designers plan the scenery for a ballet in great detail.

The scenery is built by skilled carpenters, and painted by scenic artists.

Props, such as the cradle in "The Sleeping Beauty," are made in the workshops. They need to be very hard-wearing, so they last for many performances.

All Dressed Up

It was mayhem as the dancers got ready for the dress rehearsal. The King and Queen were bickering over who should wear the largest crown. The Bad Fairy was muttering darkly in a corner, and the good fairies nearly came to blows over the sets of sparkly wings.

Bella was behaving like a real spoiled princess, complaining loudly that her tutu was too tight, when, all of a sudden, Boris appeared.

A hush fell over the room. Dressed as Prince Florimund, he looked truly magnificent.

"Gosh!" giggled Bella. "You may have to kiss me more than once. I might find it hard to wake up!"

Curtain Up!

Finally, opening night arrived.

"This is it," hissed Miss Meanie from the wings, giving the Lilac Fairy a nudge forward. "Make me proud!"

As the fairies twinkled across the stage, the magical fairytale scene came to life.

In the Spotlight

Bella and Boris danced together beautifully. By the time Boris bent over to kiss his princess awake, they had won the hearts of their audience entirely.

Watching from the wings, Miss Meanie couldn't believe her eyes. Bella was finally a prima ballerina!

Ballet Words

These are some words you might hear in ballet class:

arabesque The dancer balances on one leg, with the other raised behind.

barre Handrail used to balance while exercising.

pas de deux A dance for two people in ballet, usually male and female.

pirouette A particular way of turning on one leg, usually en pointe.

en pointe (point work) Dancing on the tips of the toes, using specially hardened shoes.

prima ballerina Principal female dancer in a ballet company.

rosin White sticky powder used to stop shoes slipping.

solo A dance for one person.

spotting A method of fixing your eyes on one spot when turning, to avoid dizziness.

tutu Ballerina's skirt made of many layers of net.